THE LEGEND OF FRANGO® CHOCOLATE

ROBERT SPECTOR

DOCUMENTARY BOOK PUBLISHERS CORPORATION
KIRKLAND, WASHINGTON

TABLE OF CONTENTS

Library of Congress Cataloging-in-Publication Data
LC# 93-073903
Spector, Robert
The Legend of Frango Chocolate
ISBN 0-935503-14-5
1. History
2. Cookbook
3. Recipes–desserts

Author: Robert Spector
Publisher: Barry Provorse
Copy Editor: Judy Gouldthorpe
Cover and book design: Nancy Gellos Studio

FOREWORD

Few candies are extraordinary enough to merit their own book. But Frango® Chocolate is different; it's a legend. Like salmon and espresso, Frango Chocolate is one of the great tastes of the Pacific Northwest.

For more than seven decades, Frango Chocolate has been the most popular candy in this region, where it is practically synonymous with the holidays. That's why The Bon Marché decided to make every effort to save Frango Chocolate for the Pacific Northwest. Because we were successful, a tradition will endure.

The Bon is adding another chapter to the candy's legend with Café Frango, in our downtown store. Drop by when you're in Seattle. There's a Frango milk shake waiting for you.

Robert DiNicola
Chief Executive Officer
The Bon Marché

P.S. Since cooking with Frango Chocolate is almost as much fun as eating it, we've included a few tasty recipes for your pleasure. Enjoy.

INTRODUCTION

Frango® Mint Chocolate is considered one of the first great commercial icons of the Pacific Northwest, along with the B-17 airplane and the Kenworth truck. It is

this region's most popular candy and a favorite of chocolate lovers from virtually every corner of the world. As befits a legend, Frango Chocolate has long been coated in myth and misinformation; the exact year of creation and the origin of the

name have been lost to history. This book comes as close as possible to the definitive story. One thing we know for sure is that during Frederick & Nelson's final days, frantic Frango Chocolate fanatics, concerned that a tradition was coming to a close, triggered a "run" on the candy.

Why all the fuss? Frango Chocolate sparks a deep emotional response in the soul of the people of the Pacific Northwest. After all is said and done, the legend of Frango Chocolate is almost as much about the folklore of this *place* as it is about the candy's *taste*. Longtime Frango Chocolate lovers instinctively understand this. All it takes is just one bite.

A FROZEN DESSERT

The year 1918 was an eventful one for Seattle and the world. The world war had helped the city to develop into one of the leading shipbuilding centers in the country, and sparked an economic boom that saw the population grow to more than three hundred thousand.

A few years earlier, D. E. Frederick, the surviving founder of Frederick & Nelson (his partner, Nels Nelson, had been dead for several years), foresaw the boom and decided to move his store from the city's retail center at Second Avenue and Madison Street—where The Bon Marché was also located—to Fifth Avenue and Pine Street. Shock waves from fellow retailers greeted the plan, which was branded "Frederick's Folly" by journalists, businessmen and financiers. Pine Street and Fifth Avenue was

D. E. Frederick

considered the suburbs—a semi-residential district that was a half-dozen blocks away from other retailers and lacked a single neighboring large building.

Frederick & Nelson, 1918

But Frederick had thoroughly studied the flow of traffic and the direction in
which the city was expanding. He was convinced that Seattle would eventually
be built up northward and eastward—away from the steep grades of its hills—
toward the more level ground. The astute merchant was confident that the new
site would create a natural traffic bottleneck through which the people of the
expanding residential districts would have to pass in order to reach the retail,
wholesale, manufacturing and banking areas at the south end of town,
along Second Avenue.

On September 3, 1918, F&N workers completed the move to the new six-story, 412,900-square-foot building, which was Seattle's largest retail space until 1922, when The Bon Marché opened its new store at Fourth and Pine.

F&N workers celebrated the end of a long weekend's move from the old store to the new one.

Frederick's grand and elegant Tearoom quickly became Seattle's most sophisticated spot for lunch, and the place to go for noontime fashion shows featuring Paris designer originals. A popular item on the Tearoom menu was a frozen dessert called Frango, which was available in maple and orange flavors.

(According to a trademark document from the U.S. Patent Office, the name Frango was first officially used on June 1, 1918.)

Fashion shows were staged in The Tearoom every Wednesday at noon during the fashion seasons, and twice a year F&N presented a special showing of Paris originals.

To call the dessert "rich" would be an understatement. It was made with 32 percent butterfat—more than three times the butterfat content of most ice creams. The silky smooth confection melted in the mouth and coated the taste buds. Wanda Ashley, who as a college student worked in the Frederick & Nelson candy kitchen in 1926, described Frango's consistency as 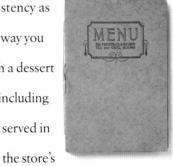 "flaky." "You didn't eat it with a spoon the way you do ice cream," she recalled. "You ate it with a dessert fork." Eventually, the Frango dessert line—including pies, ice cream sodas and milk shakes—was served in  the store's soda shop and later the popular luncheon meeting place, the Paul Bunyan Kitchen.

Where did the name "Frango" come from? There are many stories floating around the Pacific Northwest, but no one knows for sure. It's probably an acronym, with the "Fr" representing Frederick's. But the "ango" is open to interpretation. Some speculate that it was taken from the tango—a big dance craze of the era that was popularized in America by Vernon and Irene Castle.

Contrary to legend, there is no record that Frango Chocolate was ever called "Francos," and no basis to the oft-repeated story that the name was changed to Frango Chocolate because animosity toward Spain's Generalisimo Franco caused sales to drag. Franco did not rise to power until the late 1930s.

To set Frango Mint
Chocolate apart from
Frederick & Nelson's other
chocolate candies, Frango Mints
were packaged in distinctive
green and white tins.

On the other hand, another Pacific Northwest department store introduced a candy product called Francos after World War II, but was soon ordered to change the name.

In April 1921, Frederick's opened its own in-store candy kitchen, which "began with little more than four walls and sunshine," according to a March 1931 article in the employee publication, *Between Ourselves*. To oversee the candy making, Frederick's hired Ray Clarence Alden, a Seattle native who had been involved in the candy business most of his life. (His parents' West Seattle candy store was a popular spot for local kids with change jangling in their pockets.) Under Alden's direction, Frederick's candy kitchen made and sold all sorts of hard candies and hand-dipped chocolates.

Frango creator Ray C. Alden and his son, John, in 1931. (Photo courtesy of John Raymond Alden)

In about 1928 or 1929, someone decided that Frederick's should expand its candy offerings with a chocolate mint truffle. Alden and his crew went through numerous tasty trials and errors before arriving at what they felt was the ideal recipe, according to original crew member T. Frank Foss, who was interviewed by *Seattle Post-Intelligencer* columnist Sally Raleigh for a 1976 article entitled "Ray Alden Was Inventor of Frango Chocolates." The secret recipe formula called (in part) for chocolate from cocoa beans grown on the African Coast and South America, triple-distilled oil of Oregon peppermint and 40 percent butter.

Like any new product, Frango Mints, as it was called, needed a promoter. Luckily, it had one in-house in the person of a smooth-talking bon vivant named Gil Ridean, or "Gilbert Leroy Ridean, beloved son of Lydia C.," as he often introduced himself. Ridean had managed a couple of soda-fountain restaurants—

the Pig 'n' Whistle and the Puss 'n' Boots in Oakland and Seattle—before he was hired in 1927 by D. E. Frederick to manage the F&N Food Division, which included the candy kitchen, bakery, Tearoom, fountain lunch and cafeteria.

Gilbert L. Ridean (right) with Seattle restaurateur Walter F. Clark, posing at a mock backdrop at a restaurant trade convention. (Photo courtesy of Mary Clark Crabtree)

"Gil was a great raconteur," recalled Mary Clark Crabtree, whose father, Seattle restaurateur Walter F. Clark, was Ridean's closest friend. Ridean told *Seattle Times* reporter Don Duncan in a 1979 interview that when he built the Puss 'n' Boots in about 1916, he wanted the best interior decor possible. So he hired "a Mr. Boeing, who was trying to start an airplane business." Ridean added that, "Boeing later told me he had only one airplane on order in his shop. Doing our woodwork kept his men busy."

In 1916, Boeing's business was slow and, to keep its twenty employees busy, the company built cabinets for Ridean's Puss 'n' Boots. Shown is a Boeing model HS-2L fabricated in 1919, when business was down and the company built bedroom furniture to keep busy.

Frango mint chocolate truffles were originally packed in square tin containers along with other Frederick & Nelson candies, but caused such an immediate sensation that they were soon packed in their own special green and white containers. (With the metal shortages of World War II, tin was replaced by cardboard.) The cans were the same size as today—eight ounces—but priced considerably lower: fifty cents a tin. "If you wanted to do something for somebody, and you didn't want to make it a big gift, you would buy Frango Mints," remembered Wanda Ashley.

Frederick & Nelson's candy makers made Frango Chocolates by hand until the invention of its patented Frango machine in 1958.

Frederick's ice cream maker Oscar Skau, who began working in the ice cream factory in the late 1920s, credited Ridean with making Frango Chocolate a success. "He was a helluva good promoter. He took that piece of candy and he made it into something." The combination of Alden's tasty truffle, Ridean's salesmanship and Frederick & Nelson's reputation as a purveyor of fine products was the ideal recipe for what became the quintessential Pacific Northwest confection.

Oscar Skau, supervisor of ice cream production for Frederick & Nelson, formulated Frango Mint Ice Cream right after World War II. "I was fooling around with chocolate syrup and mint and then I took a whole bunch of Frango mints and melted them and made them into a block," Skau recalled. "Then I shaved them off and put them in the ice cream. At our taste panel, which we had every week, they decided to call it Frango Mint."

Soon after its Seattle debut, Frango Chocolate was destined to also become the quintessential Chicago confection. On June 12, 1929, D. E. Frederick sold Frederick & Nelson (for $6 million) to Marshall Field & Company. Some months later, when the impact of what would become the Great Depression began to be felt, Ridean and the F&N candy makers went to Chicago to introduce Frango Chocolate to Marshall Field, which had been in the food business since 1890 and had been manufacturing its own candies since 1915.

Marshall Field executives were "about as depressed as the economy," Ridean recalled for *Seattle Times* reporter Don Duncan. "They hoped Frango would help bail them out. They put out some two hundred thousand letters to customers, asking them to try the new confections." Frango Chocolate (which included both mint and mocha flavors) was an instant hit. Soon the Marshall Field candy makers produced their own midwestern interpretation of the Frango Chocolate recipe.

Frango Chocolate was such an instant hit that it kept the F&N switchboard busy with orders.

For the next sixty-three years, F&N made and sold Frango Chocolate west of the Mississippi, while the Chicago retailing giant supplied the rest of the country. Thanks to F&N and Field's, Frango Chocolate became one of the best-selling premium chocolates in the United States.

During the 1930s, F&N introduced Filbertos, a Frango Chocolate made with filberts (or hazelnuts), then Jamaicas, a rum-flavored Frango Chocolate mint "tangy-er than Frango Mints...dressier than Filbertos... as delectable and delicious as tearoom frango dessert," as described by a 1937 newspaper advertisement. A 1938 Marshall Field employee newsletter raved about the "secret recipes owned by Frederick & Nelson sold by the ton, not only to Seattleites, but also to epicures in every corner of the world."

Frederick's small candy kitchen—consisting of a couple of gas ranges and copper kettles and a half-dozen workers making hand-dipped chocolates—couldn't keep up with the demand for Frango Chocolate. So Ridean asked his good friend Joe Vinikow, who owned and operated the Parisian Candy Company

on Washington Street in Seattle, to make Frango Chocolate for Frederick's. Vinikow's factory, which was equipped to produce virtually any type of candy, made gumdrops, hard candy, peanut brittle and candy bars for Frederick's Candy Shop, as well as for other Seattle stores such as Bartell Drugs and G.O. Guy.

F&N greatly enlarged its candy kitchen operation and staff when the store was expanded in 1952.

"We could do more in fifteen minutes than ten hand-dippers could do in a day," recalled Pete Vinikow, Joe's son. "I can remember Frederick's truck backing up to our loading dock and workers loading trays of unlabeled chocolate mint truffles into the truck," which then took them to Frederick's for hand-wrapping and packaging. In 1943, Frederick's acquired Vinikow's Parisian Candy Company factory, in part because it possessed a large sugar quota—a valuable commodity during the rationing days of World War II.

The Frederick & Nelson delivery fleet

Gil Ridean retired from Frederick & Nelson in 1948 to take over Von's Café on Fourth Avenue, which was the inspiration for the current Von's on Pine Street. He continued his love affair with the chocolate mint truffle he helped make famous. "Sure I still eat them," he told the *Seattle Times*. "Doesn't everybody?"

In August 1952, Frederick's completed a $10 million expansion of its downtown store, adding four and a half new floors, which gave it ten floors above the ground level and two below. On the tenth floor, the company built a modern candy kitchen that could turn out more than five hundred thousand pounds of Frango Chocolate a year. The kitchen remains there  today, but few people have ever seen it. Several years ago, when a charity auction offered a tour of the candy kitchen plus the winning bidder's weight in Frango Chocolate, it drew a top bid of several thousand dollars.

Like Coca Cola, Frango Chocolate is produced by a recipe and a manufacturing process that are closely guarded secrets. This much is known: The chocolate filling is melted and then blended with one of a variety of flavors such as mint,

almond, rum, peanut butter, latte, espresso, raspberry or orange. After it is blended in vats and partly cooled, the chocolate is poured onto a conveyor belt, where it flows in a flat brown river at the rate of one foot per minute, slowly solidifying at a temperature of 42 to 44 degrees.

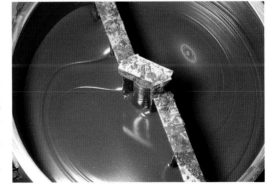

Frederick's Fine Chocolates is the largest user of chocolate in the Pacific Northwest, and one of the largest handmade-candy kitchens in the country.

The solid sheet moves through the secret Frango machine, where it is cut into the familiar shape by heated wires and blades. (The patented machine was invented in 1958 by a group of F&N people led by Vice President E. Lamont McDonald.)

Each piece is drenched with a creamy chocolate coating in what resembles a miniature car wash, then cooled.

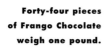

Forty-four pieces of Frango Chocolate weigh one pound.

The candies are then individually checked for quality, twist-wrapped in biodegradable cellophane at the rate of

two per second,
and hand-packaged
in the familiar
hexagonal boxes.

Pride of workmanship is an obvious
ingredient in the making of the
product. "We have a tradition of
quality," Clare Taylor, the candy kitchen's product supervisor, told the
Daily Journal-American about the sentiment shared by her coworkers.

"We feel that Frango
is our personal product."

From 1982 to 1991, Frederick's went through four owners and steadily lost business. At the end of 1991, as it became apparent that Frederick's would not survive Chapter Eleven bankruptcy, the people of the Pacific Northwest feared that they would no longer be able to enjoy their beloved Frango Chocolate. To fill the potential void, a few local candy companies and retailers began producing and advertising Frango look-alikes.

In response to unprecedented demand that Christmas season, the candy factory churned out chocolate eighteen hours a day. Nevertheless, when shoppers descended upon Frederick & Nelson to scoop up Frango Chocolates, they encountered empty shelves and the lingering aroma of chocolate. The *Seattle*

**Frango Chocolates are packaged
by hand for that personal touch.**

Times reported, "A line of customers wound up the block and around the corner at the downtown store Saturday morning, waiting for the doors to open and Frango Chocolate to go on sale. The store had to open ten minutes early to keep the crowd happy. The first sixty or seventy cases of the brand new Raspberry Frangos (about $21,000 worth) were gone in about thirty minutes."

The following February, the *Seattle Post-Intelligencer* described a scene in which "the cash registers throughout the store remained stagnant, except downstairs in the Arcade, where the dollar signs were ringing loud and clear as Frango-bearing customers clamored around the candy counter." A customer who had squirreled away several containers said, "I want to get these now because they aren't going to be around much longer."

By the spring of 1992, all Frederick's stores were closed. The sole surviving operation of this once-vast retail dynasty was the candy kitchen, which continued producing Frango Chocolate like a heart pumping oxygen.

Marshall Field and its parent company, Dayton-Hudson, Inc., challenged F&N's right to continue to make and sell the candy, which was sold through various western department stores, because F&N no longer fit the required label of "quality department store" chain. (Frederick's agreement with Marshall Field required it to operate a minimum of four stores.)

Several companies emerged as suitors for the Frango Chocolate license in the Pacific Northwest. From out of the pack of suitors came The Bon Marché, a department store chain that had been as much a part of the Pacific Northwest as Frederick & Nelson. Like F&N, The Bon was founded in 1890, but unlike its Pine Street competitor, The Bon was lucky enough to have had consistent and far-seeing ownership ever since it was sold in 1927 to Hahn Department Stores, which evolved into Allied Stores Corp., today called Federated Stores Inc.

In September 1992, "after nearly four hours of talks, sweetened with plenty of mint and raspberry Frango Chocolates," reported the *Seattle Times*, The Bon Marché and Marshall Field hammered out a license agreement.

"Our driving force was to be able to roll Frango Chocolates out by Christmas time. That was crucial," said Arthur D. Jackson, Jr., The Bon's legal counsel and vice president for government affairs.

The Bon gained permission to sell Frango Chocolate products at its stores in Washington, Oregon, Idaho and Montana, and to use Frango Chocolate recipes, packaging and "other intangible rights." The Bon also purchased whatever rights and license agreements F&N had, including the design of the Frango Chocolate box.

In a separate agreement, Frederick's candy kitchen, operating as Frederick's Fine Chocolates, Inc. (a division of Citicorp Interim Services, Inc., a wholly-owned subsidiary of Citibank, N.A.), would continue producing the product for The Bon.

"There will be Frango Chocolates for Christmas 1992," F&N's chief operating officer, David Taylor, announced to a relieved Frango-loving public.

"Frango Chocolates are a legendary Northwest treasure," said John Buller, The Bon's senior vice president of sales promotion and marketing, in the *Seattle Times*. "We are excited about the opportunity to preserve the Frederick & Nelson legacy for Frango mint lovers."

On Thursday, November 5, 1992, Seattle Mayor Norman B. Rice proclaimed "Frango Day" at The Bon Marché. The ceremony began at the corner of Fifth and Pine, where Mayor Rice and executives from The Bon, F&N and the Frango candy kitchen climbed into a horse-drawn carriage, which was ushered by a brass ensemble down Pine Street and into The Bon store at Third and Pine. Kevin McAfee, a candy kitchen employee, performed a rap song he wrote about Frango Chocolate. That day, Frango Chocolate became available in most Bon Marché stores, and a Pacific Northwest institution was saved.

On September 29, 1993, Café Frango, a sweet shoppe and bakery, was opened on the Metro level of the downtown Seattle Bon Marché store.

At first Frango Chocolate was eaten one piece at a time. Then it became the secret ingredient in treasured family recipes. A few of the best Frango creations follow.

Glassware: Kosta Boda

The Classic Frango Milk Shake

Ingredients

1   pint premium vanilla ice cream

$1/4$ cup Mint Frango Chocolate Sauce

1   pint whole fresh milk

Preparation

Chill two 16-ounce tall stemmed glasses. Place ice cream, Chocolate Sauce and milk in a blender and blend until very smooth. Pour into chilled glasses and serve at once.

Servings: 2
Preparation time: 5 minutes

Sun Valley Orange Frango Mousse

Servings: 6
Preparation time: 20 minutes
Standing time: 3 hours

Ingredients

24	Orange Frango Chocolates (1 box)
6	Tbsp. heavy cream
5	large eggs, at room temperature, separated
$^1/_2$	tsp. orange extract
1	Tbsp. grated orange zest

Preparation

Chill six 8-ounce serving goblets. Melt chocolate in a double boiler over hot, but not boiling, water; blend with heavy cream, then set aside until cool. In a large bowl blend egg yolks, orange extract and orange zest with an electric mixer at high speed until smooth and very light (about 3 minutes); add melted chocolate and blend until creamy. In a medium bowl, whisk egg whites until soft peaks form, then slowly fold into chocolate mixture. Divide the mousse among the chilled goblets and serve, or cover with plastic and refrigerate. Garnish with whipped cream topped with a hint of orange zest or a very thin slice of fresh orange.

Option

Substitute Espresso Frango Chocolate or Raspberry Frango Chocolate for Orange Frango Chocolate.

Mr. Al's Frango Cookies

Preparation

Preheat oven to 350 degrees Fahrenheit. In a large bowl, cream butter and sugars with an electric mixer until light and smooth. Stir in eggs and vanilla, and beat until well blended. In another bowl, blend flour, soda and salt until thoroughly mixed. Add flour mixture to egg mixture and stir until well blended. Gently fold in Espresso Frango Chocolate (or the Frango Chocolate of your choice). Cover dough and refrigerate for 30 minutes, then roll cookie dough into 1 $^1/_4$-inch balls and set about 1 $^1/_2$ inches apart on a cookie sheet lined with waxed paper. Bake on middle rack of oven for 8 to 10 minutes, or until cookie tops begin to crack. Remove from oven and place on cooling rack until firm.

Ingredients

$^1/_2$ lb. unsalted butter, at room temperature
1   cup firmly packed dark brown sugar
$^3/_4$ cup sugar
2   large eggs, at room temperature
2   tsp. vanilla extract
3   cups all-purpose flour
$^3/_4$ tsp. baking soda
$^1/_2$ tsp. salt
$^1/_2$ lb. Espresso Frango Chocolate, coarsely chopped

Option

$^1/_2$ cup coarsely chopped hazelnuts, roasted and skinned

Option

Fold in nuts, or for very adult cookies, try $^1/_2$ cup coarsely chopped whole-bean Rum Frango Coffee. Be creative, use any Frango Chocolate flavor you like. Our favorite is Rum, and we add 1 tablespoon of fresh grated orange zest, which really makes the cookie special.

Servings: 48 large cookies
Preparation time: 20 minutes
Baking time: 8-10 minutes
Standing time: 30 minutes

Seattle Frango Coffee Mocha

Ingredients

1 Tbsp. Rum Frango Chocolate Sauce (or flavor of your choice)

$1^1/_2$ oz. espresso coffee

$^1/_2$ cup steamed milk

Preparation

In a chilled mixing bowl, whisk cream until it forms soft peaks. Add vanilla and sugar and whisk until stiff. Put Chocolate Sauce in the bottom of a pre-warmed mug. Brew espresso and mix with chocolate sauce. Steam milk with espresso maker (140-150 degrees Farenheit). Pour milk over espresso-chocolate mixture, then top with whipped cream and serve immediately.

Option

Use melted Frango Chocolate in place of chocolate sauce, and fresh brewed coffee instead of espresso and steamed milk. It's lighter and faster, but it's still full of Frango chocolate flavor.

Servings: 1 or more
Preparation time: 5 minutes

Poached Hood River Pears with Raspberry Frango Chocolate Sauce

Ingredients - poached pears

2   Tbsp. fresh lemon juice

6   medium Bosc or other firm pears

2 $^1/_4$ cups sugar

$^1/_2$ tsp. vanilla extract

1   cinnamon stick

$^1/_2$ cup grated white chocolate

Preparation

Put 2 cups cold water and lemon juice into a large bowl. Peel pears (leave stems on) and immediately place in lemon water. In a large saucepan, combine 9 cups cold water, sugar, vanilla and cinnamon stick and bring to a boil. Drain and add pears, cover, reduce heat to low and simmer until pears are tender when pierced with a fork (about 20 minutes). Remove from heat, uncover and cool to room temperature. (Poached pears can be refrigerated overnight.)

Servings: 6
Preparation time: 30 minutes
Standing time: 2 hours

*Ingredients - Raspberry Frango Chocolate Sauce**

    24 Raspberry Frango Chocolates (1 box)

   $^1/_2$ cup heavy cream

Preparation

Whisk together raspberry chocolates and cream in a double boiler over simmering water until smooth. (Sauce should lightly coat a spoon. If too thin, add more chocolate.) Remove from heat, cover and refrigerate for at least 2 hours, or until the mixture is thick enough to hold a shape.

Final assembly

Drain and pat dry pears. Cut pear bottoms flat so they will stand straight. From the base, remove the core of each pear with a melon-ball cutter, then fill the hollow with raspberry chocolate sauce. Reheat the remaining sauce and use some of it to coat the bottom third of the pears; roll each pear in grated white chocolate. Distribute the remaining sauce among 6 chilled flat plates and stand a pear on each one. Garnish with chopped white chocolate, fresh raspberries and a sprig of mint.

* As a tasty shortcut, try Frango Chocolate Raspberry Sauce. It's ready to serve and stores well in the refrigerator.

Rum Frango Freeze

Ingredients

1	lb. Rum Frango Chocolate (2 boxes)
6	large egg yolks, at room temperature
1	Tbsp. vanilla extract
3/4	tsp. ground cinnamon
2	cups heavy cream

Servings: 6
Preparation time: 20 minutes
Standing time: 3 hours

Preparation

Chill six 8-ounce serving goblets. Melt chocolate until smooth in a double boiler over hot, but not boiling, water; set aside until cool. In a large bowl, blend egg yolks, vanilla and cinnamon with an electric mixer on high speed until smooth and light, then add chocolate and mix until completely blended. Pour heavy cream into a chilled mixing bowl and whisk until soft peaks form. Stir 1/4 of the whipped cream into the chocolate mixture, then slowly fold in the remaining whipped cream. Divide into chilled goblets, cover with plastic wrap, and let stand in freezer for a minimum of 3 hours before serving. Just before serving, garnish with whipped cream topped with a cinnamon stick.

Option

Substitute Latte Frango Chocolate for Rum Frango Chocolate, and the dessert will be lighter in flavor and color.

The Thumbprint Cookie

(they're not just for kids anymore)

Servings: 36 large cookies
Preparation time: 20 minutes
Baking time: 15 minutes

Ingredients

$^1/_2$	lb. unsalted butter, at room temperature
$^2/_3$	cup sugar
2	large egg yolks, at room temperature
1	tsp. vanilla extract
2	cups flour
1	tsp. baking powder
1	tsp. ground cinnamon
1	Tbsp. grated lemon zest
	Pinch of salt
1	cup finely ground hazelnuts
18	pieces Frango Chocolate, cut in half

Preparation

Preheat oven to 350 degrees Fahrenheit. Cut and fit waxed paper to a cookie sheet and set aside. In a large bowl, blend together butter and sugar with an electric mixer at high speed until light (about 3 minutes). Add egg yolks and vanilla and beat at medium speed until just blended (do not overmix). In a separate bowl mix together flour, baking powder, cinnamon, lemon zest and salt. With a wooden spoon stir dry ingredients into egg-mixture and blend until smooth. Roll dough into $^3/_4$-inch balls and roll in hazelnuts. Place balls on the cookie sheet about 1 $^1/_2$ inches apart. Dent the center of each cookie with your thumb, then fill with $^1/_2$ piece of your favorite Frango Chocolate. Bake on middle rack of oven for 10 to 15 minutes, or until cookies feel crumbly. (These cookies do not brown, so don't overbake.) Remove from oven and cool on wire rack.

Evergreen Mint Frango Chocolate Brownies

Ingredients

1	Tbsp. flour
12	pieces Mint Frango Chocolate
10	Tbsp. unsalted butter, at room temperature
1	tsp. vanilla extract
1	Tbsp. instant coffee (dry crystals)
4	large eggs, at room temperature
$1/2$	tsp. salt
2	cups sugar
1	cup flour, sifted
1	cup finely chopped walnuts

Servings: 24 brownies
Preparation time: 20 minutes
Baking time: 20 minutes
Standing time: 30 minutes

Preparation

Preheat oven to 350 degrees Fahrenheit. Line the bottom of a buttered 9- by 11-inch metal baking pan with waxed paper and butter the paper; dust the pan with 1 Tbsp. flour. Add chocolate to the top of a double boiler set over hot, but not boiling, water, and stir until smooth. Remove from heat and thoroughly blend in butter, vanilla and coffee, then set aside to cool. In a large bowl, blend together eggs and salt with an electric mixer until very light, then slowly add sugar and beat until fluffy (about 15 minutes at medium-high speed). Slowly stir chocolate mixture into batter, then gently fold in flour and nuts (do not overblend). Turn batter into prepared pan and spread evenly. Bake for 20 minutes, or until a toothpick inserted in the center comes out slightly moist and edges begin to crack. Remove from oven and cool for five minutes. Turn onto a cookie sheet and remove waxed paper; then return to cleaned pan and cool completely (overnight, or for 30 minutes in a freezer). Frost with Frango Buttercream Frosting and garnish with chopped nuts.

Frango Buttercream Frosting

Ingredients

$1/2$ lb. Frango Chocolate
      (any flavor you choose)

2   Tbsp. unsalted butter,
    at room temperature

$1/2$ cup heavy cream

2   Tbsp. corn syrup

*Servings: Enough to cover
     1 unfilled layer or flat cake
Preparation time: 20 minutes*

Preparation

    Put chocolate, butter, cream
     and corn syrup in the top of a
double boiler over hot, but not
boiling, water. When ingredients
   begin to melt, remove from heat
   and whisk until thoroughly blended.
(To stiffen, set pan in ice and
    continue to whisk.)

ACKNOWLEDGMENTS

This book represents the combined talents of many people: designer Nancy Gellos; editor Judy Gouldthorpe; publisher and Frango Chocolate connoisseur Barry Provorse; Mark Gordon, director of the Bon Marché Photo Studio, and his staff; and The Bon Marché's executive chef Frank Brennan and Chef Al Wood, the cookie king, who created the Frango dessert recipes especially for this book.

Our gratitude goes to the Museum of History and Industry for many of the historic images in this book; and to Jean Godden, who mentioned in her *Seattle Times* column that we were seeking the origin of Frango Chocolate: almost two dozen people responded.

Finally, thanks for the support and creative freedom given to us by the Bon Marché's Robert DiNicola, John Buller, Gary Yiatchos, Carole Couture and Jan Weaver.

Robert Spector

Seattle, Washington